The Ultimate Coffee House Business Plan

Sandaleen Khan

The Ultimate Coffee House Business Plan

Cafe-Au-Lait Business plan

LAP LAMBERT Academic Publishing

Impressum/Imprint (nur für Deutschland/only for Germany)
Bibliografische Information der Deutschen Nationalbibliothek: Die Deutsche Nationalbibliothek verzeichnet diese Publikation in der Deutschen Nationalbibliografie; detaillierte bibliografische Daten sind im Internet über http://dnb.d-nb.de abrufbar.
Alle in diesem Buch genannten Marken und Produktnamen unterliegen warenzeichen-, marken- oder patentrechtlichem Schutz bzw. sind Warenzeichen oder eingetragene Warenzeichen der jeweiligen Inhaber. Die Wiedergabe von Marken, Produktnamen, Gebrauchsnamen, Handelsnamen, Warenbezeichnungen u.s.w. in diesem Werk berechtigt auch ohne besondere Kennzeichnung nicht zu der Annahme, dass solche Namen im Sinne der Warenzeichen- und Markenschutzgesetzgebung als frei zu betrachten wären und daher von jedermann benutzt werden dürften.

Coverbild: www.ingimage.com

Verlag: LAP LAMBERT Academic Publishing GmbH & Co. KG
Dudweiler Landstr. 99, 66123 Saarbrücken, Deutschland
Telefon +49 681 3720-310, Telefax +49 681 3720-3109
Email: info@lap-publishing.com

Approved by: Islamabad,Bahria University,2010

Herstellung in Deutschland:
Schaltungsdienst Lange o.H.G., Berlin
Books on Demand GmbH, Norderstedt
Reha GmbH, Saarbrücken
Amazon Distribution GmbH, Leipzig
ISBN: 978-3-8454-2125-4

Imprint (only for USA, GB)
Bibliographic information published by the Deutsche Nationalbibliothek: The Deutsche Nationalbibliothek lists this publication in the Deutsche Nationalbibliografie; detailed bibliographic data are available in the Internet at http://dnb.d-nb.de.
Any brand names and product names mentioned in this book are subject to trademark, brand or patent protection and are trademarks or registered trademarks of their respective holders. The use of brand names, product names, common names, trade names, product descriptions etc. even without a particular marking in this works is in no way to be construed to mean that such names may be regarded as unrestricted in respect of trademark and brand protection legislation and could thus be used by anyone.

Cover image: www.ingimage.com

Publisher: LAP LAMBERT Academic Publishing GmbH & Co. KG
Dudweiler Landstr. 99, 66123 Saarbrücken, Germany
Phone +49 681 3720-310, Fax +49 681 3720-3109
Email: info@lap-publishing.com

Printed in the U.S.A.
Printed in the U.K. by (see last page)
ISBN: 978-3-8454-2125-4

1 Contents

PART 1:BUSINESS PLAN

1

PART II: MARKETING PLAN

Dedicated to my mother, who was always a source of Inspiration to me.

PART 1: BUSINESS PLAN

2 INTRODUCTION

<u>Name of the Business</u>: Café au lait

<u>Address:</u> Sector F-7/2, Jinnah Super, Islamabad, Pakistan

<u>Nature of business</u>

Café au lait (a French word which literally means coffee with milk) will be the first French Coffee house located in the F-7/2, Jinnah Super, Islamabad.

The coffee cafe will offer a variety of choices to the customers. Coffee and tea of all sorts will be offered. The choices of coffee will range from espresso to latte, from regular flavor to raspberry mochas. The teas will range from English, to flavored varieties. Juice, soda, and non-alcoholic beverages also will be available.

The breakfast menu will feature croissants, muffins, bagels, donuts, french pastries, fruit filled crepes, etc. Lunch and dinner will feature sandwiches, pizza, finger fish with french fries, salads and soups.

<u>Statement of Financing Needed</u>

A 100% Equity Financing will be used to launch Cafe au liat because taking a loan from the bank might involve a lot of hassle and also interest rates might rise in future due to deteriorating economic conditions. Investor A will bring int

the business a total of 700,000 (35%), Investor B will invest 500,000 (25%) and Investor C and D will invest 400,000 (20%) each.

The above mentioned amount Rs 2,000,000 will be used to start the operations of Cafe au liat. This will include purchasing of ice-cream cycles, purchase of new small bus for delivering ice-creams and cakes to different retail outlets, purchase of production machines, advance payment for using land and building on rent, payment for getting our business registered, marketing expenditure etc.

Once Cafe au liat start's operating, its performance will be reviewed each month. All monthly expenditures will be deducted from the revenue earned to find out the net profit. Some of these expenditures will include fuel Charges, cost of Utility Bills, building rent and others. Decision regarding distribution and reinvestment of net profit will be made with the consent of the business partners.

3 EXECUTIVE SUMMARY

The interest by consumers in the coffee cafe industry is sweeping the country. Cafe au liat is positioned to bring this to the F-7/2, Jinnah Super. To date it has been confined to the Central and East areas.

Cafe au liat will provide a friendly, comfortable atmosphere where the customer can receive quality food, service and entertainment at a reasonable price. The coffee cafe will offer a variety of choices to the customers. Coffee and tea of all sorts, will be offered. Juice, soda, and non-alcoholic beverages will also be available. Cafe au liat will serve breakfast, lunch and dinner.

The interior design of the building will focus on projecting a relaxed atmosphere. Cafe au liat will be divided into different areas. Some will have tables and chairs, another will have large antique stuffed couches and chairs, end tables, coffee tables, book shelves filled with books and magazines, tiffany style lamps and braided rugs. A PA system will be installed so that the music and entertainment can be heard throughout. A large selection of table games will be provided. There will be nightly entertainment featuring acoustic jazz, blues and folk music. On selected nights there will be poetry readings and an open microphone. The walls will be used as an art gallery and from time to time there will be an artist in residence.

The area of Jinnah Super where Cafe au liat will be located is populated with young, upwardly, mobile persons with expendable income and also surrounded by markets. This is complemented by a large number of upper middle class "Baby Boomers" who are a large portion of those persons who frequent coffee cafes.

A strength which this business will possess is the ability to change with the times. Rather than limiting the future opportunities by having a small area, Cafe au liat will have 3,525 square feet of space and a kitchen designed for flexibility.

As the fad of coffee cafe fades, Cafe au liat will be able to change to a full course restaurant or whatever the situation calls for. The advertising and promotion will take a number of avenues. First, flyers will be distributed in the neighborhood then ads will be taken out in all of the major bulletins in the area. Since Cafe au liat will be the first union restaurant in the state, ads will be placed in all of the union newsletters. Ads will also be placed in the target areas of the United' Grocery, and the local neighborhood newsletters. For businesses in the area, menus will be distributed and ordering will be available by fax. A Customer mailing list will be developed with a calendar of events being mailed on a monthly basis.

Cafe au liat will be operated as a joint partnership. There will be private investors. However, these investors will be silent

investors with a payoff of investment within three years. These investments will be paid twice-yearly in equal installments including interest. The total needed capital for Cafe au liat is Rs. 2,160,000. Owner's cash contribution is Rs. 2,000,000 and other investors and family members is Rs.160,000. The amount needed in loans is Rs.90,800 for equipment, Rs.70,000 for remodeling, and Rs.80,000 for operations. This is a total of Rs.240,800.

4 INDUSTRY ANALYSIS

4.1 Future Outlook and Trends

Coffee growth looks promising in light of increasing food service sales which is creating a coffee culture in Pakistan. This is coupled with the increasing number of instant coffee products available in the retail arena. Tea on the other hand will perform better as a refreshing drink to help consumers cope with their busy lifestyles and rising stress levels in the forecast period. While Lahore's coffee scene is growing, Karachi's, Pakistan's largest city, has exploded. In Karachi alone there are are currently 31 different coffee companies and CafÃƒÂ © Coffee Day, India's largest retail coffee shop chain, plans to open 19 more outlets across Pakistan in the next 12 months after the success of its first venture in Karachi. Moreover International Chains like Gloria Jeans has also opened 4 outlets in Pakistan due to the emerging coffee market in Pakistan.

Economy

Culture

The Indian-subcontinent, in particular Pakistan, has been a tea-drinking country since before the British made tea popular in the West. Tea is consumed throughout the day and often served accompanied with samosas and various sweets like golabjamins or cookies. Most offices have chai wallas or tea boys who serve workers multiple cups of tea during the course of the working day. On average, each Pakistani consumes about a kilo of tea a year, making approximately 140m kg of tea for a population of about 140 million.

But all of that is changing. In the last few years Pakistan has seen an explosion in coffee lounges and cafes. Some are like your traditional Starbucks just serving coffee and snacks, while others are more all-inclusive cafes, serving coffee accompanied by proper meals. Pakisatn is an emerging

7

market for coffee.Coffee culture has been so fast in spreading its wings with new coffee outlets opening left, right and centre in Pakistan. These coffee shops have played an important role in introducing coffee to the masses in Pakistan.

Now that coffee awareness has grown to such an extent, tea might finally have competition. Younger generation in Pakistan definitely prefers coffee over tea. This is not only because coffee is more hip than tea but also because coffee is more helpful in keeping energy levels going longer than tea ever has been. Professionals in Pakistan who need to be on the go for long hours are fast quitting the frequent tea breaks with fewer coffee breaks.In markets in Pakistan there are many varieties of instant coffee mixes available. Ironically now in Pakistan making tea is considered more difficult then coffee, now that is how intensely coffee culture has taken over. In addition usage of coffee in everyday products especially bakery products has become very frequent.

In the more mature markets, the patterns of consumption have changed markedly over the last 10-12 years. The traditional, lower quality coffee products such as instants, are being replaced by roast and ground coffee (drips, plungers etc) and of course Espresso based drinks (cappuccino, latte, espresso etc). Fresh roasted coffee has many advantages over the instant coffee. It is more flavoursome and more importantly has a greater link back to where it originally came from. This means that customer awareness is also on the increase- bringing into the spotlight the actual paper trail of where the coffee comes from, who picked it and what price the grower gets from it, etc.

Wireless Technology

Coffee cafes have become establishments where people are not only drinking coffee but also surfing the Internet, working at their laptops, or communicating with friends, family, and colleagues. Wireless technology is changing the way people live. Hotspots (Internet access areas that deploy wireless technology) can be found in airports, hotels, and coffee cafes. Some offer free access while others require paid subscriptions. Offering free wireless Internet in coffee shops is sure way to boost success. People are now given the option to make a connection over a cup of coffee and/or over the Internet.

5 Analysis of Competitors

Yummy's, In Jinnah Super is one of the oldest coffee and ice cream parlours in the city.It is well known and has customer loyality.But its weakness lies in the fact it has the same old varieties that might appeal to older generation but not to younger generation that prefer changes.

Dunkin' Donuts, F-7 Markaz (Blue Area), F-10 Markaz, G-10 Markaz, etc .Its a well known coffee house,an International chain but it's donuts are losing the standardized tastes and it has limited varieties of coffee to offer.

8

Hangout, F-7 Markaz (Jinnah Super), behind Shell petrol station. A wonderful little coffee shop/sheesha bar. They serve a small selection of global and local food, and play sexy Bollywood and Egyptian videos. Posters of Jimi Hendrix, 50 Cent, Marilyn Manson and Angus Young are on the walls. One room is all men. Another for mixed couples and ladies only.Its weak point is that the ambience is targeted for younger generation only and does not cater senior citizens or middle-aged people. Some conservative people find the ambience and the whole concept of the café rather too bold.

Rakaposhi, pastry shop at the Serena, has some of the best coffee and pastries in Pakistan. Worth a visit if you just want to relax or get some work done. The Serena also offers wireless internet, so, it is an ideal place to sit and get some work done if you like.The only weekness is that it's priced very high and there are lot of security checks before entring Serena,which drives some customers away.It's target market is rather the rich segment or the Upper Middle Class.

Civil Junction, F-7/3 markaz (Gol Market) offers good coffee and an interesting array of drinks and 'mocktails'. Light snacks are also offered along with coffee and drinks. The place offers occasional live music from upcoming local bands, making it a popular hangout with the youth of the city.

Rif's café, is a small coffee shop, with "books kind" of a café that is located in Kohsar Market of F-6/3.Due to lack of Advertising and Publicity it's less known. It targets mainly foreigners.

Gelato Affairs:It is located in F-7/3, Gol Market Neighborhood: F-7, F Area .It is a coffee house and ice-cream bar.

Gloria Jeans:It is an International chain which is located in Kohsar Market,F-6/3, Islamabad.It's the toughest competitor in Islamabad.This place looks and feels like a very modern coffee house. There is a large variety of yummy-looking desserts, and a full range of coffees. The decor is very pleasant. Gloria Jean's is very different from other coffee shops as everything they sell is international. They have their own coffee beans, which are specially prepared by Gloria Jean's Australia. Everything is imported, their cup, spoons,forks. This is the only international operating coffee house [in Pakistan]. Their staff is trained by people coming in from Australia.

They have their own take on traditional drinks like lattes. One of the more tempting ones is a Chocolate Macadamia Latte, which combines hot chocolate and espresso with macadamia nut flavor. Their frozen drinks are just as interesting. They also think outside the box when it comes to frozen and blended drinks. The Frozen Coconut White Chocolate drink blends coconut, coconut syrup, white chocolate and milk together with ice.They also have a free-Wi-fi and no smoking zone.

Gloria Jean's clientele is mostly upper-class to upper-middle class, with a focus on young executives, college students, families, and foreigners.

A lot of foreigners come in to Gloria Jean's. Many of them say: "It's the closest thing to Starbucks"' The only weak point is that some items on the menu fail to meet customer expectations.

Espresso Lounge :Neighborhood:Blue Area, 10-12 Trade Centre,behind 7th Avenue Jinnah Super,Islamabad. Coffee Bar and Lounge Espresso Lounge is for everyone who loves the coffee there. For those who crave something other than coffee they have a selection of traditional and herbal teas, fresh juices and delicious fresh-fruit smoothies. Their chef mixes up a feast of delicious sandwiches, pastas and mouth-watering salads to keep you going throughout the day. And, once again for the health-conscious, we offer an array of weight watcher's sandwiches and wraps. Espresso lounge has consistantly been recognized for its all organic quality product, its unique designer friendly atmosphere but mostly its eclectic clientele. It's a cool hang-out where you could work, rest and play. Espresso Lounge marries together the love of design, all things beautiful and our passion for the world's number one drink - coffee.

Masooms: It is located in F-11 markaz,Islamabad.You can treat yourself on any occasion with death by chocolate, New York cheese cake, mochas, java, blueberry and strawberry cheesecakes as well as many other delightful varieties.It is our toughest competitor in terms of goumet items and cake vaieties.Coffee and tea are also served.You can make gift boxes with vanilla toffee brownies, almond biscottis, blueberry muffins, blueberry pastries, Kentucky cake, triple chocolate fudge and a variety of other rich chocolate delicacies. Masoom's will personalize cakes for you, making special decorations, sizes and shapes. Apart from the sweet treats, you can indulge in lovely creamy chicken sandwiches, pizzas and patties. Massom's stresses on hygiene and using high quality ingredients. In addition to this, they are generous with stuffings and fillings, so you really get your money's worth.

6 Market Segmentation

For the purpose of defining the target market, the following market segments were established after researching the restaurant and cafe-going consumers and the clientele of already established competitors.

Marital and Family Status
Single
Single with Dependants
Married
Married with Children
Married with Dependants

While evaluating their consumer market the conclusion was that the ideal consumer's economic profile will be:

- *Upper Middle Class*
- *Elite Class*

While the age demographics will be:

- *Students and Youngsters*
- *Professionals*
- *Families*
- *Mature Consumers*

Gender and Ethnic/Religious Background was researched to have minimal or no effect on the choices concerning coffee made by consumers and their patronage of coffee houses.

Economic Profile

To achieve the vision of Cafe au liat *"We will dominate every place in Pakistan where coffee is sold"* we shall continue using the same method of slow-roasting coffee beans that is unique to Cafe au liat to this day. The focus will be on quality control at every stage of the coffee making process from bean to cup. Unlike any other coffee company in the Pakistan, Cafe au liat has its own roastery to ensure their unique blend is perfect every time. The customer can order a cup of Cafe au liat today; it is made skillfully by hand rather than by the automated coffee machines used by major competitors.

Age demographics

Students and Youngsters i.e. young men and women in the age bracket of 16-24 years are estimated to form 30% of the target market. This group will patronize Cafe au liat for the ambiance and the prestige as well as the delicious menu. Due to the burgeoning "Coffee Culture" in Pakistan, the youth is flocking towards coffee houses and cafes as their latest 'Watering Holes'. The luxurious environment and the image of class associated with Cafe au liat is bound to attract this group and make them a significant fraction of Cafe au liat potential clients.

Professionals belonging to all careers and in the age bracket of 24 – 45 years are anticipated to form 45% of the future clientele. These will be up and coming, dynamic persons who will appreciate the mouth-watering menu, expeditious service and serious atmosphere. Cafe au liat is the ideal environment for efficient lunches and meetings from casual to semi formal to formal.

Families: Cafe au liat menu caters to a variety of tastes and aims to satisfy all kinds of customers. Though a lesser percentage than students and professionals, we hope that consumers with families will make up 10% of the potential patrons. Cafe au liat's wide array of scrumptious choices is designed to draw consumers of all ages: the melt-in-your-mouth luscious desserts will without doubt make children love them while their parents can also enjoy the unique, delicious coffee; Making Cafe au liat a complete family experience.

Mature Consumer: Our mission is selling the best quality coffee with best services at every privileged place in Islamabad. The trade mark is the exceptional quality and first class flavor. Who is better than a matured, experienced veteran with discerning taste to appreciate the finer points of Cafe au liat? The management hopes that matured consumers will comprise 15% of the potential clientele.

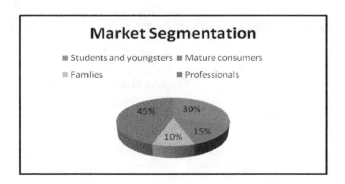

Market Segmentation

Students and youngsters ■ Mature consumers
Famlies ■ Professionals

45% 30%
10% 15%

7 Industry and Market Forecasts

The coffee business has boomed in recent years, especially with regards to specialty coffees. The market for specialty coffees has grown as consumers become more educated about espresso-based drinks and how they are made. According to a National Coffee Association Annual Drinking Trends Survey, specialty coffee consumption has risen from 9 percent in 2000 to16 percent in 2004. Every day, more than half of the adult population drinks coffee, 108.9 million people. While fast food chains are growing at a rate of 2 percent each year, coffee chains grow more than10 percent annually.

Customizing according to interests in local markets is a way for coffee shops to create loyalty and increase sales. Espresso and other specialty coffees are becoming popular in quick service - restaurants. While consumption of gourmet coffee has remained steady, purchases of espresso beverages have risen from 4 percent to 7 percent. Gourmet coffee had been the strongest growing part of the market, but recent studies have shown that that the trend toward occasional drinkers is continuing while espresso drinks continue to rise in popularity.

Specialty coffees seem to be most appealing to younger adults. The 25 - 34 age group accounted for one-quarter of specialty coffee orders in 2000 and only 10 percent of the regular coffee orders. Those 18 – 34 years old have increased their specialty coffee purchases at table service restaurants in the last two years. One-third of regular coffee orders are placed by consumers 65 and older, while that group accounts for less than 10 percent of specialty coffee orders.

Adults Who Drank Gourmet Coffee or Specialty Coffee [*]

Gender	Percent Index
Men	47-98
Women	53-102
Age 18-24	9-73
Age 25-34	15-80
Age 35-44	21 100
Age 45-54	21 111
Age 55-64	14 117
Age 65 and above	20 116

Index Indices above 120 or below 80 generally indicate the percentages were notably above/below expected levels, based on population figures.[*] In the past seven days.

Half of restaurant orders for coffee (regular and specialty) are placed during the breakfast/snack mealtime. One fourth of specialty coffee orders are during the p.m,snack mealtime, more than during lunch or dinner. Quick service restaurants, which include coffeehouses and coffee shops, account for 75 percent of all specialty coffee orders, but only account for half of all restaurant occasions for any type of coffee.

Cafe au liat traffic grew 8 percent in 2000, while the overall growth in the quick service segment was only 1 percent. The specialty coffee retail sector is estimated to be Rs8.4 billion, and for prepared beverages, Cafe au liats report an average of Rs170,643 in gross sales.

There is a growth in the number of cafes and restaurants that serve flavored hot drinks and the different types of imported coffee in Pakistan. This trend benefited on trade sales and people in the upper income urban group flocked to these food service outlets at the expense of retail sales. Food service tea consumption of average cup per day grew to 5 as compared to last years cups per day of 4. Whereas Coffee consumption grew to an average 3 cups per day as compared to 2 cup per day since the last 3 years. This was due to increasing number of women working in cities and increasing in number of cafes in urban areas of Pakistan.

Hot drinks experienced slower growth in 2008 than in previous years due to changing weather conditions, specifically rising temperatures, so the people are drinking less hot drinks. The real value growth is seen to be less dynamic compared to the reviewed period. Consumers are seen to trade down and remain more conservative in their purchasing decision which hampers real price growth. Tea as always enjoys the highest consumption level with teabags performing the best due to rising use of tea bags in offices. Coffee saw good growth in fresh coffee due to increasing coffee shops that use fresh coffee more now than any other type of coffee.

Even in the days of serious political crises nothing could hinder these companies from growing and yet they became successful. A major reason behind this is the nature of the product (coffee) that is affordable by anyone no matter what income group he or she belongs to. The demographic changes as well didn't have any negative impact on this industry since coffee target all genders and age groups.

8   DESCRIPTION OF VENTURE

Mission statement

To provide a friendly, comfortable classic french cafe atmosphere where the customer can receive quality food, service and entertainment at a reasonable price.

Business goals

Our goal is to be the Cafe au liat of choice for people of Islamabad, downtown business workers, tourists who visit the city, and students, by providing a higher quality experience and exquisite ambience than any other competitor. As a result, we intend to create Cafe au liat that quickly achieve profitability and sustain an attractive rate of return (20% or more annually) for our investors. Furthermore,we would like to create a business and working environment where both the customer and employee are treated with dignity and respect.

The specific goals of the business are:

Profit - Personal income in excess of Rs.105,0000 per year within three years

Clientele - Create a base clientele of persons who live nearby and work in the area. These people will like a relaxed atmosphere where they can "hang out"

15

Employees - Competent employees (at least 51% from low-income neighborhoods) who are committed and loyal

Keys to Success

The keys to our success will be:

- Superior-tasting products and a diverse menu.

- A relaxing, upscale classic french interior design

- Prime site selection with an upscale affluent population, year-round tourist activity, heavy pedestrian traffic by the site, a dynamic student population and a concentration of local businesses

- A market that exposes Café au lait to high-profile "trend-setters" and "key influencers"

- Ongoing, aggressive marketing

- Highly trained and friendly staff

- Multiple revenue streams including gift items, gift baskets and coffee gift/frequency cards in addition to coffee, pastry, chocolates, tea, juice, water and soft drinks

- A dynamic website with online sales capability

Products

Café au lait will sell high-quality specialty coffee beverages, tea, juice, water, soft drinks, pastries, chocolates and gift items. Despite being an upscale Cafe au liat, our prices are in line with the leading national chains.

9 The Café au lait Menu

The Café au lait menu sets us apart from other Cafes, giving us a competitive edge.

- We offer six groups of drinks—coffee, tea, Italian sodas, smoothies, juice and cocoa—with several choices within each group. This enables us to provide more variety than our competitors while keeping the preparation of the drinks easy to execute.

- We are taking advantage of the immense popularity of flavored drinks and Chai tea by offering a product mix that includes items the other Cafes don't carry as well as more familiar drinks.

- We are the only Cafe to have a wide range of gourmet hot cocoa.

- Café au lait offers several smoothie drinks and Italian sodas.

- We carry the highest quality fresh juices.

Prices have been determined after a thorough analysis of all food costs for every item in each drink. In some cases, an average price has been calculated and applied to all similar drinks in order to keep the menu from confusing the customer. Prices typically range from Rs 80 to Rs 200.

Coffee and Espresso Drinks

Coffee flavors

Coffee Krunch Blend
Riviera Roast
French roasted Cofee
Hazelnut Creme Coffee Costa Rican Coffee
Guatemala Coffee
Jamican Blue coffee
Colombian Coffee
French Roast Coffee
Italian Roast Coffee
Irish Creme Coffee – Decaf
Swiss Chocolate Coffee

These coffees will be priced at Rs200 for Regular and Rs250 for a Large cup. These Coffee flavors will only be available over the weekends and will be added to the regular menu if a favorable customer response is observed.

Espresso Types

Name	Description	Regular	Large
Espresso	A double shot of straight espresso.	Rs.120	Rs.140
Caffe Americano	Espresso combined with hot water, a gourmet brewed coffee.	Rs.110	Rs.140
Cappuccino	Espresso with a smooth topping of milk foam.	100	130
Caffe Latte	Espresso combined with steamed milk, topped with a small amount of velvety milk foam.	110	140
Caffe Mocha	A Caffe Latte combined with Ghirardelli chocolate, topped with whipped cream and chocolate shavings.	135	160
Espresso Macchiato	A straight shot of espresso topped with a spoonful of rich milk foam.	120	150
Espresso Con Panna	A straight shot of espresso topped with a generous dollop of whipped cream.	120	150
Espresso Latte Breve	Our famous latte made even more creamy with half and half.	130	150
Espresso "Red Eye"	Espresso combined with our gourmet coffee of the day to get your day going.	130	160

Coffee drinks

Name	Description	Small	Large
The Banana Nut Java	Coffee. Warm milk. Banana, macadamia nut and vanilla syrups. Topped with whipped cream and cinnamon dusting.	Rs175	Rs250
The Cafe Milano	Coffee. Warm milk. Amaretto and vanilla syrups topped with whipped cream and almonds.	Rs160	Rs220

Flavoured espresso drinks

All flavored drinks feature quality Monin and Ghirardelli syrups.

Name	Description	Regular	Large
Vanilla Cappuccino	Cappuccino made with vanilla flavored milk foam.	Rs 150	Rs200
Vanilla Latte	A Caffe Latte with vanilla essence added.	165	210
White Chocolate Latte	Espresso, white chocolate flavoring and steamed milk topped with velvety foam and white chocolate shavings.	200	250
The 50/50 Latte	Espresso. Vanilla and orange syrups, steamed milk and whipped cream topping.	210	260
Th Raspberry Mocha Latte	Coffee. Raspberry and chocolate syrups. Half and half. Whipped cream topping.	200	250
Chai Latte	Espresso. Chai. Steamed milk and whipped cream.	160	190

Hot cocoa drinks

All hot cocoa drinks are priced at Rs 265

Name	Description
French Vanilla Cocoa	Hot cocoa with vanilla and whipped cream.
White Chocolate Cocoa	Hot cocoa with white chocolate and whipped cream.
Chocolate Truffle Cocoa	Rich dark hot cocoa with whipped cream topping.
Holiday Spice Cocoa	Rich hot cocoa and holiday spices. Topped with whipped cream.
Peppermint Cocoa	Rich chocolate and refreshing peppermint. Topped with whipped cream.
Ovaltine	Ovaltine Chocolate Malt and milk.

Smoothies

All smoothies are priced at Rs 215

Name	Description
The Espresso Chocolate Malt	A chocolate malt for grown-ups.
The Double French Chocolate Smoothie	Very chocolatey!
The Mocha Smoothie	An all-time favorite.
The Vanilla Smoothie	Rich natural vanilla flavor.
50/50 Smoothie (Orange and Vanilla)	A 50's favorite.

Teas

Iced tea

Classic American Iced Tea - **Rs 80 Small, Rs 1100 Medium, Rs 150 Large**

Hot tea - Rs 100 Regular

Earl Grey
English Breakfast
Peppermint
Herb Apricot
Earl Grey Lavender
Darjeeling
Formosa Oolong
Golden Flowers Herbal
Herbal Lemon
Tropical Green

Chai teas (hot or ice blended)

Chai Original (regular or decaf):	Rs 50 Regular Rs 80Large
Vanilla Chai:	Rs 60 Small Rs 80 Medium Rs 110 Large

Juices

Name	Description	Regular	Large
Fresh squeezed orange juice(seasonal)	Made from fresh oranges	Rs 100	130
Old-fashioned Lemonade	Made fresh daily from Pleasant County lemons.	85	100
Genesis Juice	Protein Boost, Green Machine, Mango and Guava.	125	140
Apple Juice	Made from the export quality apples	100	130
Mango Juice (seasonal)	Made from fresh mangoes	110	140

Italian Sodas

Iced Italian sodas

Sparkling spring water, flavoring and ice. Blended or on the rocks.Medium Rs 85 and large RS 110

Orange Soda
Strawberry Soda
Lemon Soda
Cherry Soda
Raspberry Soda
Cream Soda (made with half & half)
Peach Soda
Kiwi Soda
Apple

Speaciality   Italian   Sodas

All Rs 80.75 Regular, Rs120.50 Large

Name	Description
The Dreamsicle Soda	Sparkling spring water, ice, half and half, vanilla and mandarin orange syrups.
Cherry Vanilla Soda	Sprite, ice, cherry and vanilla syrups.
The Chocolate Soda	Our version of an egg cream.

Other Drinks

	Description	Price
Nestle Water	Mineral Water	Rs60
Soft drinks	Pepsi, Coke, Sprite, Mountain Dew, Marinda,Fanta,7-Up.	25
Green Tea	Made from leaves imported from China	55
Red Bull	Energy Drink	120
Custom made drinks	Orange Cream, Ginger Ale, Vanilla Cream and Key Lime	130

Pastries and other gourmet items

	Price
French chocolate pastries	255
Fresh scones, hot from the oven.	200
Bagels	190
Brownies	110
Blueberry Muffins	195
Croissants	160
Black Forest chocolate-covered espresso beans	145
Chocolate, Strawberry and Vanilla Donuts	65

Deli Items

Item	Price
Sandwiches: Chicken, Turkey, Roast Beef	Rs 175
Hot and Sour Soup, Chicken Corn Soup, Thai Soup, Tomato Soup/cup	Rs 145
Chicken Tikka Pizza, Chicken Fajitta,(regular)	Rs.510
Finger Fish with French Fries/plate(7 pieces)	Rs 350
Café au lait Special Mixed Salad	Rs 160

Cakes

Death by chocolate cake
Trip chocolate fugde cake
Ice-cream cake
Strawberry ripple Cake
lemon Tart cake

Cakes are priced at Rs. 130 by half slice.

Ice-creams

Daniel Quinlan	Mike Storm
Uncle Ed	Itai
Ellmist	Tedius Zanarukando
Muriel Gottrop	Dungodung
Oliver P	Owlpostforever
utcursch	Joku Janne

Cheese Cakes

All Cheesecake will be sold by the half slice. Price per half slice is Rs 225. Whole cheesecakes will be available for purchase at a price Rs 675.

FRESH STRAWBERRY
WHITE CHOCOLATE
RASPBERRY TRUFFLE®
FRESH BANANA CREAM CHEESECAKE
CHOCOLATE SILK AND SATIN CHEESECAKE

TIRAMISU CHEESECAKE
CHOCOLATE MOUSSE CHEESECAKE
VANILLA BEAN CHEESECAKE
TRIPLE CHOCOLATE CHIP
KAHLUA COCOA COFFEE CHEESECAKE
PASSION FRUIT PINA COLADA
DULCE DE LECHE CARAMEL CHEESECAKE
WHITE CHOCOLATE CHUNK MACADAMIA NUT
CHOCOLATE TUXEDO CREAM CHEESECAKETM
DUTCH APPLE CARAMEL STREUSEL
BROWNIE SUNDAE CHEESECAKE
CHOCOLATE PEANUT BUTTER COOKIE-DOUGH CHEESECAKE
KEY LIME CHEESECAKE
LEMON RASPBERRY CREAM CHEESECAKE
CHOCOLATE RASPBERRY TRUFFLE®
GERMAN CHOCOLATE CHEESECAKE
CHOCOLATE CHIP COOKIE-DOUGH CHEESECAKE
STICKY CHEWY
CHOCOLATE PECAN CHEESECAKE
LEMON MOUSSE CHEESECAKE
SOUTHERN PECAN CHEESECAKE

CHOCOLATE PECAN TURTLE
CHERRY
BLUEBERRY

Services

Along with the regular routine services rendered by the waitersm, Wi-Fi connection in the café would also be offered for all customers .

Size of business

Café au liat will start its operations from Islamabad and for a year it will only concentrate in gaining popularity in this city. Later after gaining financial strength it will expand its operations to other cities like Rawalpindi and Lahore. A double storie building covering an area of less than one "Kanal" will be hired on Rent where all the machines will be installed for the staff to work and produce coffees, cakes, etc.

Office Equipment and Personnel

One computer will be given to each Director to record important company information. For example the Finance Director will use it to prepare monthly and yearly financial statements. Production department will record the production of each product line and the performance of production employees in their system. Quality Control Director will keep records of performance of suppliers to ensure supply of good quality raw material. Marketing Director will keep record of the money they are investing in promotional activities and their future plans. The Distribution Director will record information about outlets that are carrying company products and the new outlets that he has explored for supplying company products. The HR director will use computer to record how many leaves an employee has taken, when he arrived at the work place, how many hours he worked and what would be his salary at the end of the month. Computers would also be provided to the CEO and the MD. Other office equipment would include a single printer which will be linked to all the computers at the workplace. Telephone and Fax Machine will also be used at the workplace. Back up of all the company data will be maintained on CD's.

10 PRODUCTION PLAN

Café au lait will be located Jinnah Super Market, The cafe will utilize the newly remodeled main floor next to the building the building, which has 3,000 square feet of usable space.There is a substantial amount of start-up equipment that will need to be purchased. Most will be financed with the Standard Chartered loan.

Location

Cafe au liat will be the first free "connected" cafe in the Jinnah Super Market area.

Located on the corner of 15th Street and Main Street in Jinnah Super, Cafe au liatwill be situated in the most high traffic area of sector F7. The cafe will move adjacent to the local library and bookstore Saeed book bank.

Facility

The Front plaza that will house Cafe au liat has been updated to facilitate new building codes and improved technological devices. Vaulted ceilings will add to the quaint charm of the coffee shop. The cafe walls will be painted in warm tones to enhance the calm environment of the coffee shop; however, the large pillars that hold up the ceiling will be decorated with art from local artists. The furniture will be shallow wooden tables and chairs with a glossy finish

The cafe will utilize the main floor of the building, and cater to the office employees and nearby students. The main floor has 3,000 square feet of usable space.

Below is the complete interior design for the Coffee House:

Plants - climbing ivy, terracotta pots, geraniums spilling over the side of a planter and topiary's

Bistro Table & Chairs - either black or white iron or wooden to seat 2-4 people.

Art - Chalkboards with French (words) menu items. These can be made easily by putting a picture frame around an existing chalkboard. These signs can either by hung on a wall or displayed on a standing tripod. Use colored glass bottles as accent pieces.

Awnings - To create the cafe' look without a whole lot of maintenance, just use a simple cafe umbrella, Indoors or out, this will add an element of drama to the space.

Lamps or Candle Holders - To add the ambience of romance, candles are a must for your table or the counter tops. Lampshades should be dark colored and beaded.

Wall Art - Coffee & Food - What a better way to communicate a cafe style than to add food art to your walls. Espresso, coffee, latte art and posters can be displayed to coordinate with your color scheme or select complimentary art with a Paris theme to complete to look of your room.

11 Operating Equipment

In order for Cafe au liatto begin operations, there are many items that will need to be purchased. Follows is a list of items necessary to begin business:

3 Bunn-O-Matics - Rs72,500
3 Cappuccino Makers – Rs32,000
2 Computers – Rs66,600
Routers & Networking – Rs24,500
Printers & Misc. Hardware – Rs58,000
Furniture & Fixtures – Rs200,000
Counter & Kitchen Equipment – Rs320,000
Signage - Rs53,000
Flatware & Tableware – Rs200,500
Leasehold Improvements - Rs100,000
POS System – Rs345,000
Total Purchases - Rs147,2100

General Operations

Cafe au liat will be open for operation the following hours:

Monday to Thursday: 7 a.m. to 9 p.m.

Friday and Saturday: 10 a.m. - 1 a.m.

Sunday: 10 a.m. - 4 p.m.

Cafe au liatwill comply with all the federal, state, and local laws and regulations. The house will obey all the worker's compensation rules.

12 OPERATIONAL PLAN

Descripton of company's operation

The goal of the operational plan is to Keep cost of goods sold at or below 30%and to provide customers with prompt and courteous service.

Objective

- Provide initial training for all employees

- Hold monthly employee meetings

- Have an open door policy for employee suggestions

- Implement the use of the Business Plan systems

- Purchase and use the Food Fax software package

- Have clearly defined job descriptions and duties

- Have an employee policy handbook

- Do employee reviews every six months

- Customer suggestion box

- Design kitchen and service area to be efficient.

Flow of orders for goods and/or services

The product will be distributed in the restaurant by food servers. The food will be cooked on site, except for some of the baked goods. Some of these, such as croissants will be purchased in the raw frozen form and baked daily.

When a customer enters Café au lait they will be greeted by a hostess who will seat them and provide them with menus. A server will greet them and give them water and the menu card. The server will inquire what they would like to drink. If the drink is either tea or coffee, that will be prepared by the chef. The coffee order will be given to the waiter in cash or credit card, which will be rung up on the register.The server will deliver the drinks(coffee,shakes,etc) and then take the food order if the customer is ready. The server will take the food order and give to the Head chef. The cook will prepare the food, in the order given. The server will prepare the salads, desserts, hot and cold soups and other items. The cook places the finished food on the window. The server must pick the food up within two minutes. The food is placed on the table and the server will ask if there is anything else which the customer needs. The server will check all the drinks and replenish water, ice tea and plain coffee. The server will ask if the customer needs another drink. Specialty drinks are not refill items. The server will familiarize the customer with the operations of Café au lait. They will explain to the customer that a number of table games are available if they wish to play. The server will let the customer know about the reading room and present them with a schedule of events. The customer will always be asked if they would like dessert or an after dinner coffee. The server is responsible for checking on the customer in a timely manner. This should be done in an unobtrusive manner. The server will maintain the tables in a clean and sanitary condition. Dirty dishes and plates must be removed immediately. Condiments must be kept full and the containers clean.

The Head Chef is responsible for cooking and preparing all dishes not prepared by the server. The orders will appear on the computer monitor and the cook will prepare them according to the order given. The cook and their assistants are responsible for preparing all items in the morning such as the soups for the day, slicing meat, making specialty items and other dishes for the day. The assistant cooks are responsible for the prep work of all items for the servers and the cooks. This includes stocking all supplies, cutting cheese, fruit, salad items, ice, filling soup tureens, etc.

Cleanliness is required above all else. The servers will keep all of their work areas clean at all times. Spills must be cleaned immediately. After each shift, servers will check the side work chart and have it finished before they leave. This work will be checked by the shift supervisor. The cooking area will be maintained in a clean and sanitary manner. All areas will routinely be wiped down and swept. The cooks and assistants will also have side work which must be completed before leaving. The dishwasher is responsible for keeping the dishes washed and helping with busing the tables if needed. The dishwasher is responsible for mopping the kitchen floor. All employees must read and be knowledgeable of health regulations and follow those rules. Training will be provided by Café au lait.Hands must be washed on a routine basis. Smoking is not allowed.

The servers will be required to present a clean appearance. A uniform consisting of an eggshell white polo shirt with Café au liat logo, forest green walking shorts or long pants, black sneakers and black ankle socks. The servers must be polite, friendly, and helpful, not only to the customer but to the other staff as well. At no time will employees be allowed to discriminate by remarks, actions or jokes.

Technology Utilization

Cash Register

The cash register system will be Quix 3000 Touchscreen. The built-in system software uses single or multiple remote printers, and reports and tracks data terminal to terminal, or throughout the network. Produces management reports for system, terminal, or revenue center; current and/or to-date totals for:

- Employee/cashier balance reports

- Employee tip reports

- Time period sales analysis

- Detailed or summarized menu item sales analysis

- Detailed or summarized sales group and category   analysis

Pricing

The food price will be in the moderate range and comparable to other coffee houses in the area. The cost will be determined by not only what the going rate in the area is but also by the percentage of actual cost of the food. The price will not only be competitive, but the food will be tasty, well presented, and large portions will be served in a relaxing atmosphere where the customer will be comfortable. The image projected by the pricing will be that the customer will be getting a fair value for their money; that they do not need to be rich to eat at Café au liat and anyone can afford to come in. They will be able to use the books and games. In the evening, they will be able to listen to the live entertainment.

During the day, music will be played over the PA.

Credit terms will be offered only in the form of credit card service, such as Visa, MasterCard and Discover. Many people who eat out prefer to pay with credit cards, whether it is to keep track of expenditures or for a work expense account.

The cost of the food will be based on a set percentage. Restaurants traditionally keep food costs between 26% to 32%. Based on the type of food to be served and the delivery system, the percentage for Café au liat will be an average of 30% of the actual cost of the food. In order to accomplish this, Food Fax software will be utilized. The software contains the following features

32

such as combination of days and sales mix can be sequenced to follow "Z" tape order for fast data entry.

Inventory Accounting System

Calculates cost of goods, provides shelf-order inventory forms, receiving logs, compares actual usage to average usage by item, ranks highest over and under use items. Tracks vendors, allows look-up by name or vendor item codes. Automatic distribution of invoice amounts to general ledger account numbers. Purchase and transaction recap reports, inventory level control reports, price history and fluctuation reports.

Recipe Costing and Sizing

Plate and batch recipes instantly costed as prices change. Sizing and modeling capabilities.

Menu Analysis

Complete menu and sales analysis reporting. Evaluate menu performance, run products by contribution. Product cost reports available by day or any combination of days. Sales mix can be sequenced to follow "Z" tape order for fast data entry.

Ideal Use/Perpetual Inventory

Tightest possible method of inventory control compares actual use to ideal use by item and computes variance. Includes ability to run perpetual inventories and track batch recipe production variances.

Bid and Purchase Order

Built-in bid pricing system allows entry of vendor bids and automatic selection of best price available. Shopping list feature, automatic PO creation, price history reports and more.

POS Interface

Import sales mix data directly from almost any cash register. POS system or polling package.

Accounts Payable Interfaces

Export purchases to accounts payable system.

13 MARKETING PLAN

Pricing

The food price will be in the moderate range and comparable to other coffee houses in the area. The cost will be determined by not only what the going rate in the area is but also by the percentage of actual cost of the food. The price will not only be competitive, but the food will be tasty, well presented, and large portions will be served in a relaxing atmosphere where the customer will be comfortable. The image projected by the pricing will be that the customer will be getting a fair value for their money; that they do not need to be rich to eat at Coffee Circus and anyone can afford to come in. They will be able to use the books and games. In the evening, they will be able to listen to the live entertainment. During the day, music will be played over the PA.

Credit terms will be offered only in the form of credit card service, such as Visa, MasterCard and Discover. Many people who eat out prefer to pay with credit cards, whether it is to keep track of expenditures or for a work expense account. All prices take into consideration the cost of material, 25% for food and 45% for beverages. Coffee will be sold in two sizes, with prices ranging from Rs 110 to Rs 260. Flavors will be available at an additional charge of Rs 50. Espresso, cappuccino, mocha, and other specialty drinks will be available in two sizes and will cost Rs3.75 and Rs6.50.

Cheesecake will be sold by the half slice. Prices range from Rs2.75 to Rs4.00. Whole cheesecakes will be available for purchase in a price range of Rs15.00 to Rs20.00.

Sandwiches will be sold for various prices, depending on the meat chosen. A veggie sandwich will be the lowest priced sandwich at Rs2.50. The highest priced sandwich will be the prosciutto and provolone on a wheat croissant. It will sell for Rs6.75. All sandwiches are sold deli-style. All soft drinks and juices will be sold for Rs1.25

Promotion

Promotion above and below the line will be used to make Cafe au liat a popular company. Due to limited financial resources, customers will be informed about this new venture through a TV ad which will run on Cable TV and not on big channels like Geo, ARY etc initially. At present Cable operators offer around about 7 movies on demand channels which are very popular amongst people in Islamabad. So the ad will run during the intervals and small trailers will also move on the downside of the screen to remind people about this venture. Huge emphasis would be given on making the advertisement i.e. "the message that it has to portray". Care would be taken of the fact

that the ad is persuasive and attracts people towards consuming the products that
are offered. Advertisement through Radio i.e. FM channels will also be done. Apart from this, fliers

will be used to advertise the venture. Colorful attractive fliers containing persuasive information about the company and its products will be distributed in busy areas e.g. schools. These fliers will also be distributed in residential areas in almost all the sectors of Islamabad. Posters of our new venture will be pasted in all business areas especially outside bakery shops, utility stores etc. Small banners will be placed across Islamabad on all streets light towers especially on busy roads like 9th avenue, 7th avenue, Blue area etc.

Slogans and Punch line will be critically examined before their selection bearing in mind their importance in building customer retention of the advertisement. An emotional appeal will be made to the customer through slogans and other advertisement information. Sponsorship and Prize schemes are the other ways through which promotion will be done. Focus would be given to sponsoring events organized by students in the universities and colleges e.g. seminars, marketing events etc to catch the attention of general public and the higher officials from different professional fields who are invited as guests in those events. Prize schemes like lucky draws will also be held to popularize the venture and increase sales.

Hence gradually as the venture will become popular advertisement strategy will be upgraded. TV ad will be run on most popular channels like GEO and ARY. Print media like newspaper and magazines will be used to promote our products and in other words promotion will become more aggressive as time will pass.

14 Product Forecasts

Café au lait intents to offer 14 flavors of ice-creams named as Black Current, Chocolate Chip Mint , Marsh Mellow, Napple Syrup, Bubble gum ice-cream, Cotton Candy, Peanut Butter, Jello, Cashew nuts, Chocolate Fudge, Cinnamon, Tico Rice, Chocolate with cookies and Coffee. These flavors would be available in cups, 0.5 liter and 1 liter paper packing, 1.5 and 2.5 liter tubs and also in the form of ice-cream cakes. The Production department will be held responsible for Research and Development. They will be held responsible for bringing in new ideas from the international and local market. They would be allowed to do experiments. Failure will be allowed only if they come up with something really beneficial later on. In other words a huge responsibility will be laid on the shoulders of this department to introduce new product lines. Customer surveys will also be used to make changes in the product line by including new products.

15 Controls

Performance of the venture and each of its products will be reviewed after every 3 months to apply product mix expansion or product mix contraction strategy. The company will identify which product line (cups, liter packs, tubs, Cakes) qualifies for being recognized as the most important SBU of the firm. That product line will then receive most of the company resources. Those products that will not perform well even after modification will be excluded from the product line. New flavor would also be introduced based on the customer demand.

Performance of the manufacturers will be reviewed e.g. how many hours they worked compared to how much they had to work, did they waste any raw material during production etc. Inspection will take place regularly to ensure that no one deviates from the quality standards. Decisions will be made regarding whether to continue with the existing suppliers or not. In simple words each possible step will be taken by the management of Creamy Delights to control the operations of the company.

16 ORGANIZATIONAL PLAN

Form of Ownership

The form of ownership adopted for this particular new venture is Partnership. The firm will have two partners: Investor A and B. These partners will invest money in this venture from their own pocket which is why no debt financing will be done. They will contribute in the ratio of 60:40 with Investor A contributing the major share and the rest contributed by Invesor B. All decisions will be made with the consent of these partners. Also, there would be no hiring of management.

Identification of Partners

Names of the partners and their investment in this venture are mentioned in the first module (Introductory Page).

Authority of Principals

CEO

The CEO and Marketing Director would have a certain level of authority over the (MD) i.e. the CEO would have the power to accept or reject her proposed change ideas. Apart from this she will have a major say in hiring Directors if they are needed to be recruited in future. The CEO can also fire any person from the organization if they don't work properly apart from the MD. Other than this the CEO will approve or reject the idea of allocating funds to different departments. In simple words she will have the highest decision making power in the organization.

Marketing Director

The marketing director will be responsible for all the marketing activities that will be carried out for this venture which will mainly include its promotional campaign. The Marketing Director will design the Ad for Cafe au liatin and will emphasize on the benefits of our products. The Marketing Director will also negotiate with the Cable Operators on the rates for running this ad and regarding how many times this ad will be run. Design of Packaging Material, Fliers and Posters will also fall under his/her responsibility while printing will be outsourced and this decision will also depend on the marketing director. He/She will also decide the Slogan for this venture. He/She would also inform the HR department regarding the distribution of the fliers and the posters so that she can hire manpower for it. This director will also keep an eye on the opportunity to set the company stall in exhibitions for its publicity. Also Cafe au liatintend to sponsor events organized in universities. So this area will also be seen by the marketing director. Representatives from different universities will come and visit and then she would negotiate on the rates and make the final decision.

Managing Director,

After the CEO, the MD will have the highest authority in the organization. The MD will design the work tasks for Directors and will have the power to dictate them the changes she wants from them and will have the power to hire or fire any director along with the CEO. The MD will also have a say in decisions regarding reinvestment of profit and the CEO would not have the power to reinvest profit without her consent.

Company Directors

The company directors will enjoy authority over their subordinates. They will be in a position of hiring or firing their subordinate. They would be allowed to change their working hours. Applications of Leave from the subordinates will be accepted or rejected by them. These subordinates will be given research project e.g. the QC director might ask his subordinate to find a suitable supplier for the company. These subordinates will act upon their orders. Similarly other Directors will also enjoy these powers.

Management team Background:

Finance Director

The Finance Director will be responsible for managing the entire financial perspective of the café, from what is brought into the business to the end revenues going into the business.

HR Director

The role of Human resource director includes duties like hiring personnel, keeping in check the ongoing roles the current employees are undertaking.

Roles and responsibilities of members of organization
The CEO

As the CEO of Cafe au liat, Sandaleen would be responsible for laying the overall, long-term organizational goals of the firm. She will mainly define the long term goals of the firm taking into account what the firm wants to achieve in the long term specifically stating the position it wants to achieve and hold. She will basically be communicating these goals and objectives to the managing director who would be then communicating them to the respective department directors. All in all he would be in charge of specifying the overall organizational objectives that would form the basis for action. Also she will act as the senior representative of the company when dealing with the other parties in the long run. For Example Cafe au liatmight form a Joint venture with some other company depending on the opportunity. So it will be the CEO's responsibility to carry out meetings with them and then to finally sign the contract. Apart from this she will be responsible for making decisions regarding reinvestment of profit into the company's operations. However for this we would have to take the consent of the MD.

She will also approve or reject the proposal submitted by the Finance department regarding allocation of funds and the proposal submitted by the other departments.

Managing director

The second position in the organizational structure is that of the managing director. The role of managing director in the organizational goals is to take the very long term goals defined by the CEO and then break them down into medium term goals. Thus the overall organizational goals will be broken down into more specific goals and be communicated to the respective departments. In this way, the managing director would be assigning and co-coordinating activities of the various

38

departments in the organization to achieve harmony. Also he/she would be taking information from each Director relating to their department and then she will review that information to present it to the CEO in one report summarizing the performance of the company. He/She will act as an intermediary between Directors and the CEO i.e. she will present the demands of the Directors to the CEO regarding what problems they are facing at the workplace.

Finance Director

The Finance director will be in charge of managing the Financial Matters.His/her primary task would be to prepare financial statement for each month and then for the full year. To perform this task he will have to keep a check on all financial matters taking place on daily basis. At the end of each month he will interpret and analyze the financial performance of the company i.e. how much sales the company has achieved. Which product line and distribution method brought the highest sale? How much cost was incurred in that time period including cost of manufacturing, cost of rent, utility bills etc. At the end of each month he will review the inventory policy of the firm for its raw material and finished goods. On annual basis he will also record the depreciation incurred on Fixed Assets i.e. on the (manufacturing machines). With the help of this data he will propose the desired changes in the prices of products, in purchase of raw material to get discounts, in promotional activities etc. He will also present ways for becoming cost affective i.e. method for reducing overall cost by reducing cost of company's operation without compromising on Quality.

HR Director

The HR director will be responsible for Human Resource Management. He/She will remain in close contact with the production department to hire employees who are experienced in making coffee. He/She will organize the interview session and before that he will also be responsible for designing job specification and job description for the job of making coffee. He/She would also make policies for employees carrying out the production process. These policies would be in regard to the amount of leaves they can take, their salary, the performance appraisals that they will get etc. Similarly /she will remain in contact with the other Directors to record information regarding their subordinates. Computerized records will be maintained for employees' salary; bonuses and all this data will also be printed and kept in files.

Finance Assistant

The finance director will have one employee hired externally who would assist him in managing the financial matters. He/She will be responsible for making the basic calculations regarding sales of different products and will present that report to the finance director who will then compute the

39

total sales and analyze the performance of each product. Same method will apply to the production and other expenses.

General Manager

He/She will also overlook the shift Supervisors,Head Chef , assistant cooks, servers, hostess and the bus person along with the HR Director. He/She will be responsible for the overall management of the staff. He/She will work in conjunction with HR Directors in ordering supplies, maintaining inventory, handling customer complaints and scheduling staff. Other duties would include ensuring staff coverage for all shifts and reports to the owners.

Shift Supervisor

There will be two shift Supervisors. One from 8am-4 pm and the other from 4pm-12am. They will be responsible for the oversight of the servers, bus person and hostess on their shift. They will work under the general manager. The shift supervisor also works in the capacity of a server and is responsible for waiting on tables, taking the customers' food and drink orders and acting as cashier for their customers. They are responsible for helping to keep the serving area and the customer areas clean and sanitary. They are responsible for helping the assistant cook keep the service area stocked. At the end of their shift, they will be required to complete all side work as assigned.

Head Chef

The head Chef is responsible for cooking food served in the restaurant. They also are responsible for preparing food items in advance and seeing that the service area is kept stocked. Their responsibility is to see that the kitchen is kept in a clean, sanitary and working order. They oversee and train the assistant cook. They also ensure that quality is maintained and presentation of the dishes is exquisite and precise and orders are served on time.

Assistant Cook

The assistant cook is responsible for assisting the cook in his duties. He/she is responsible for helping to keep the kitchen clean and sanitary. When needed will help with dishwashing duties. He/she is responsible for keeping the service area stocked.

Server

The server is responsible for waiting on tables, taking the customers' food and drink orders and acting as cashier for their customers. They are responsible for helping to keep the serving area and the customer areas clean and sanitary. They are responsible for helping the assistant cook keep the service area stocked. At the end of their shift, they will be required to complete all side work as assigned.

Hostess

The hostess is responsible for greeting customers as they arrive at the restaurant and seating them. She is required to take reservations and answer the phones. Also to assist with busing tables or assisting the servers when available. Duties include keeping the lobby area clean.

Bus Person

The bus person is responsible for keeping dirty dishes off the tables. When customers leave they must clean the table and prepare it for future customers. They are to help the servers with getting non-alcoholic drinks. They also are responsible for helping the servers. They are responsible for helping the assistant cook keep the service area stocked. At the end of their shift, they will be required to complete all side work as assigned.

Marketing Assistant

One more employee other than the Marketing Director will be facilitating the operations of this department. He/She will help her Director in designing the ad for the venture. He/She will present his views regarding what should be the theme of the ad, what should be the slogans. Apart from this he will present ideas for designing the packaging material, fliers and the posters. He/she will also plan as to where the fliers should be distributed and posters should be dispatched. He/she will also set the appointments of different parties like Cable operators and Event organizers with the Marketing Director. Upon setting a stall in exhibitions he will be responsible for taking care of that stall and bringing in all the news to the Marketing Director.

QC Assistant

The QC Director would be facilitated by one more employee who would work as her subordinate. The employee would manually record the amount of raw material received from each supplier and there performance and will submit that document to the Director who will then feed it into the computer. Also if the director wants to change the supplier then his subordinate will help him out in finding out the right supplier.

17 ASSESSMENT OF RISK

Evaluate Weaknesses of Business

Following are some of the weaknesses of "Cafe au liat" which can prove to be very risky:

Intense Competition

Cafe au liatis a new venture getting launched in the market, therefore it will face severe competition from well-established International chains like Gloria Jeans and Dunkin' Donuts and local coffee

shops like Rakaposhi, Yummy's, Hangout, Civil Junction, Rifi's cafe, Gelato
Afairs, Espresso Lounge, Masooms. Therefore there is a possibility that people might neglect our coffee house because these coffee houses offer diverse flavors and varieties and each is famous for its own unique mark it leaves in customers mind. Also since we are the starters; so people would have serious doubts in their mind regarding the quality of our flavors of coffees and other deli items.

Marketing efforts might prove to be ineffective

The marketing efforts of Café au lait might prove to be ineffective if compared with those of other competitors. Café au lait will use Cable TV and FM channels to advertise their products. Both these mediums are not that popular amongst people. It is actually a risk. These mediums can prove to be successful because people do watch movies on cable especially the lower middle class but there is only a 50:50 chance of success. So marketing efforts of Café au lait might get neglected due to the marketing efforts of its competitors. Also unlike its competitors, Café au lait isn't using the newspapers for print advertisement. This is another weakness of the company as newspapers and magazine appeal to a large customer segment which might now remain unaware about this company. Similarly the other promotional material like Fliers that Café au lait is using might not prove to be beneficial since people might not take them very seriously.

High Cost and low profit margins

Initially as Café au lait will start its operations its costs will be very high as it will incur a high cost on setting up the business which would include the marketing cost, cost of purchasing Fixed Assets like land, cost of hiring employees etc. This cost will be backed up by a price lower than that of the competitor in anticipation to gain popularity. Resultantly firm will earn a low profit margin and if due to any reason people might not show interest in this company then chances of loss will be very high.

Also even if the company is successful in attracting customers, competitors might lower their prices or they might introduce an effective promotional campaign to maintain their market share, giving Café au lait a hard time to establish itself. Another defensive strategy that may prove to be a risk for Café au lait could be competitors launching the same flavors at a lower price thus, attracting more customers.

Difficult to hire Specialist Employees

Another business weakness is the fact that the new venture has limited funds as a result of which it would have difficulty hiring the best workers and staff. This is because drawing employees of other firms and outlets such as Gloria Jeans and Dunkin Donuts and our other competitors would require giving them incentives like special offers and deals in addition to at least the same pay or an increased amount to attract them toward the new firm and contribute to its running significantly. Due to lack of funds, the firm will not be able to specifically hire experts in the field or the experienced employees that could work efficiently and effectively to make the new venture an immediate success.

Question Marks on the Quality of Raw Material

As in our case, we wouldn't purchase our raw material from any registered company. Though the coffee beans will be imported, there are high chances that we will get the supplies of milk from a trustworthy milkmen and same goes for the other raw materials like vegetables and chicken and meat. This is not enough to ensure that the raw material is of best quality. Henceforth the quality of final production can suffer.

Difficult to match supply and demand of Company's Products

Even if Café au lait is successful immediately after its launch, it would be difficult for the business partners to match the supply of company's products with its demand since this would be the first time that they are running any business and their inexperience can prove to be one of the biggest weaknesses of this firm.

New Technologies

Since Café au lait is a new venture that promises new flavors of coffee and innovation to its customers with a difference, new technology would play an integral part to fulfill its commitments and obligations. Thus, to start off, Café au lait will not have ample financial resources to draw upon as it would only have a limited amount available. It therefore, would at first buy less expensive machinery to start the production process and will rely on it till it successfully establishes itself in the market. However as operations take off and the firm successfully establishes itself in the market, by developing a diverse customer base, its profits would obviously rise too. This would be the time when the new venture would be stable enough and be in a capacity to afford and invest in new technology as customers will be aware of its product and the vast amount of flavors being offered.

Consequently, the firm will regularly update its machinery and keep up with the changing technology thereafter, to provide customers with a quality product.

Contingency Plan

Due to uncertainty, it is important to have contingency plans as things not always turn out to be as planned. The new venture would also have contingency plans that would be operational when things don't work out as planned. One such plan is that if the coffee flavors offered by the café au lait don't do very well and do not generate a good response, then the our café has schemes like " Coffees of the Week": Vanilla Café au lait Blend, Riviera Roast, French roasted Cofee, Hazelnut Creme Coffee Costa Rican Coffee, Guatemala Coffee, Jamican Blue coffee,Colombian Coffee, French Roast Coffee, Italian Roast Coffee, Irish Creme Coffee – Decaf, Swiss Chocolate Coffee as flavors to be offered on the weekends only till customer response is seen as positive and favorable. As these flavors are unique and different and Pakistanis are not accustomed to it. If the other flavors are not viewed as favorable than we would remove them from the menu and make these flavors as part of the permanent menu. More over,this might create a hype at first and customers might come for these flavors specifically. All of this will be evaluated through customer comment cards and from our website.

As far as suppliers of Raw Material is concerned Café au lait will remain in contact with the alternate suppliers of gourmet products and cakes like United Bakery,Gourmet and will deal with them so that if on a particular day they don't get the supplies of the cakes and pastries from it's primary Vendor Kitchen Cuisine, then they can call those alternate suppliers to get the supplies.

18 FINANCIAL PLAN

Important Assumptions

The 20-year record of positive growth for specialty coffee drinking will continue at a healthy rate. The resilience of the coffeehouse industry to negative national and world events will continue. Despite recession and war the coffeehouse industry has shown strong growth every year for the past two decades.The quality of national chains will remain the same or decline slightly rather than improve as they standardize their stores, increase automation of espresso drinks and mass-produce the roasting process. Coffee drinks will continue to be considered an "affordable luxury." 15% minimum sales growth rate over the next three years as French Coffee becomes well known.

Pro forma Income statement

Below is a summary of income and expenses for Café au lait's first three years of operation:

	Year 1	Year 2	Year 3
Income	453,064	489,311	528,455
Less COGS:			
Material	294,392	317,945	343,380
Total COGS	294,392	317,945	343,380
Gross profit	158,672	171,366	185,075
Operating expenses:			
Advertising	19,904	21,498	23,216
Internet Access	3,666	3,810	3,965
Insurance	29,328	30,502	31,720
Professional Fees	7,464	8,062	8,706
Entertainers	4,976	5,375	5,805
Salaries & Wages	163,703	180,077	198,083
Rent	42,962	45,110	47,366
Utilities	12,278	12,888	13,532
Maintenance & Repairs	6,492	7,012	7,572
Depreciation	12,695	12,695	12,695
Total operating expenses	303,466	327,029	352,660
Operating income	(144,794)	(155,663)	(167,585)
Interest expense	14,666	45,167	83,571
Net income	(159,461)	(200,831)	(251,156)

- Sales: Month 1 of Rs 42,910 and an 8% annual growth rate (based on similar sized concepts).
- **Cost of Sales:**
- Food: 25% of sales.
- Beverages: 75% of sales.
- Operating Expenses - Based On Industry Standards, Except:
- Salaries & Wages Year 1 - Rs163,705, Year 2 - Rs180,076, Year 3 - Rs198,083 (add 16% payroll burden)
- Advertising: Estimated to average 3.7% of sales, slightly lower than a new restaurant.
- Internet Access & Cable: Negotiated with local service provider.
- A 10% growth is justified by the lack of coffee shops in the area, and because of the traffic from the shopping market. It is also assumed that as the building apartments are filled, more traffic will be present in the coffee shop.

18.1 Pro Forma Balance sheet

Explanation of Projected Balance Sheet

	Year 1	Year 2	Year 3
Assets:			
Current assets:			
Cash	5,000	5,000	5,000
Inventory	2,000	2,000	2,000
Total current assets	7,000	7,000	7,000
Fixed assets (net)	76,405	63,709	51,014
Total assets	83,405	70,709	58,014
Liabilities and equity:			
Current liabilities:			
Accounts payable	25,400	27,433	29,627
Line of credit	137,337	341,029	576,029
Notes payable	0	4,816	0
Current maturities	17,589	9,901	17,404
Total current liabilities	180,326	383,178	623,059
Long-term liabilities (net)	37,739	23,022	21,602
Total liabilities	218,065	406,201	644,662
Equity	(134,661)	(335,491)	(586,648)
Total liabilities and equity	83,405	70,709	58,014

Scale "x 000"

Inventory: Fixed at Rs500,000.

A/P: Inventory purchases.

Current Maturities & LT Debt: Loans from external parties:

Standard Chartered loan: Rs500,000 @ 10.0% over 5 years

Loan from family and friends: Rs20,000 One-pay loan @ 5.0% due month 30.

18.2 Financial Potential

Cafe au liatwill be profitable in its first year. The traffic from the local library, the corporate workers in the building it operates from, and from the busy streets will ensure a successful venture. A modest loan from the Whittaker's parents and favorable terms from the SBA will prove to be beneficial as Cafe au liatgrows and prospers.

Cafe au liatwill have sales of Rs533,764 in its first year of operation. Years two and three will have sales increases of 10%, resulting in sales of Rs576,551 and Rs622,575, respectively. Operating expenses are Rs304,136 for year one, Rs327,694 year two, and Rs353,326 year three. The results for the first three years of operation are net income of Rs36,521 for the first year, Rs42,356 for the second year, and Rs47,819 for year three.

Below is a graph displaying the French coffee House's financial position during its first three-year period:

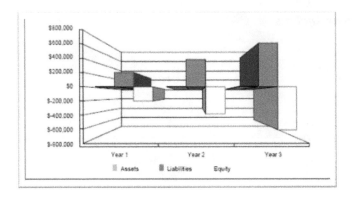

18.3 Explanation of Break Even Analysis

BREAK EVEN ANALYSIS

COGS and Expense Analysis, for the three years beginning May 2010

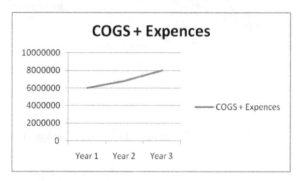

18.4 Income Analysis

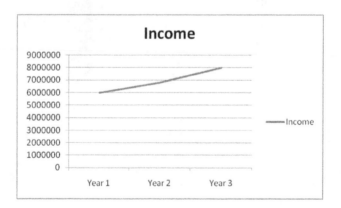

18.5 Sources and Application of Funds

The business partners of Café au lait firmly believe in Equity Financing and therefore no application of fund is required at the moment as the company isn't intending to go public or to obtain a loan from the Bank.

House Description

The unique theme of the Café au lait will bring expectations of an upbeat, cozy, and friendly atmosphere. The House's floor plan (covering 33 yards by 40 yards) and furnishings have been designed to ensure these expectations are met. The space is currently designed for a book store, but will be remodeled with a glass storefront. The interior will be unique, offering a high, decorative ceiling. The common area will have wooden coffee tables surrounded by plush chairs and sofas. On the walls, wooden tables with standard chairs will allow patrons to setup laptop computers and spread out paperwork. The walls will be painted in a warm color scheme to enhance the relaxed atmosphere. The walls will be decorated with artwork from local artists.

The floor plan will provide 3000 square feet of usable space inside in addition to some corner seating outside. Café au lait will provide an upscale atmosphere, but with competitive coffee prices.

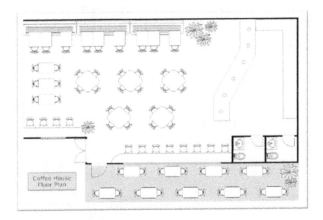

Above is draft of the floor plan as it will look upon remodel completion

19 APPENDIX

Letters

Company hasn't received any letter of appreciation from its suppliers or customers since it hasn't started its operations yet. Upon starting its operations it will keep a back up of such material.

Market Research Data

Interviews were conducted from the customers of Gloria Jeans.They were asked the following questions:

1: How often do you visit Gloria Jeans or other coffee houses outlet?

2: What's special about Gloria Jeans that you don't find at other coffee houses?

3: Are the pastries,cakes and coffee offered by other cafes different from Gloria Jeans.

4: Which flavor of coffee do you like the most?

5.Is the Ambience as important as the menu?

Lease or Contract

Café au lait has a three year agreement with the owner of the building in F-7/2,Jinnah Super,Islamabad. Till June 30th June' 2012 the company will continue its operations from that building and will pay a rent of Rs 200,00 each month which will increase by 10 % each year.

PART 11: DETAILED MARKETING PLAN

20 ANALYZE AND DEFINE THE BUSINESS SITUATION

THE SCOPE OF THE MARKET

The attractiveness of the Pakistani Market for Café au liat is slightly above average. The escalating Coffee Culture and the increase of Coffee drinkers in Pakistan show a healthy growth rate. The Technological Requirements for this particular venture in Pakistan are not too burdensome, considering the nature of the enterprise, the standard of the target market and the possession of advanced technology by Café au liat.

Although the Inflationary pressure does tend to increase and is unstable, the nature of the targeted market segments remains almost unaffected. Contracts with the suppliers, transporters and employees and other damage-control measure also protect the enterprise from serious danger. Thus the overall Market Attractiveness is above average and suitable of entry.

SALES HISTORY BY PRODUCT, CLASS OF TRADE, REGIONS

The coffee business has boomed in recent years, especially with regards to specialty coffees. The market for specialty coffees has grown as consumers become more educated about espresso-based drinks and how they are made. According to a National Coffee Association Annual Drinking Trends Survey, specialty coffee consumption has risen from 9 percent in 2000 to16 percent in 2004. Every day, more than half of the adult population drinks coffee, 108.9 million people. While fast food chains are growing at a rate of 2 percent each year, coffee chains grow more than10 percent annually.

Customizing according to interests in local markets is a way for coffee shops to create loyalty and increase sales. Espresso and other specialty coffees are becoming popular in quick service - restaurants. While consumption of gourmet coffee has remained steady, purchases of espresso beverages have risen from 4 percent to 7 percent. Gourmet coffee had been the strongest growing part of the market, but recent studies have shown that that the trend toward occasional drinkers is continuing while espresso drinks continue to rise in popularity.

Specialty coffees seem to be most appealing to younger adults. The 25 - 34 age group accounted for one-quarter of specialty coffee orders in 2000 and only 10 percent of the regular coffee orders. Those 18 – 34 years old have increased their specialty coffee purchases at table service restaurants in the last two years. One-third of regular coffee orders are placed by consumers 65 and older, while that group accounts for less than 10 percent of specialty coffee orders.

Adults Who Drank Gourmet Coffee or Specialty Coffee [*]		
Percent Index		
Gender		
Men	47	98
Women	53	102
Age		
18-24	9	73
25-34	15	80
35-44	21	100
45-54	21	111
55-64	14	117
65+	20	116

Index: Indices above 120 or below 80 generally indicate percentages were notably above/below expected levels based on population figures. [*] In the past seven days.

Half of restaurant orders for coffee (regular and specialty) are placed during the breakfast/snack mealtime. One fourth of specialty coffee orders are during the p.m,snack mealtime, more than during lunch or dinner. Quick service restaurants, which include Cafe au liats and coffee shops, account for 75 percent of all specialty coffee orders, but only account for half of all restaurant occasions for any type of coffee.

Cafe au liat traffic grew 8 percent in 2000, while the overall growth in the quick service segment was only 1 percent. The specialty coffee retail sector is estimated to be $8.4 billion, and for prepared beverages, Cafe au liat's report an average of $170,643 in gross sales.

There is a growth in the number of cafes and restaurants that serve flavored hot drinks and the different types of imported coffee in Pakistan. This trend benefited on trade sales and people in the upper income urban group flocked to these foodservice outlets at the expense of retail sales. Foodservice tea consumption of average cup per day grew to 5 as compared to last years cups per day of 4. Whereas Coffee consumption grew to an average 3 cups per day as compared to 2 cup per day since the last 3 years. This was due to increasing number of women working in cities and increasing in number of cafes in urban areas of Pakistan.

Hot drinks experienced slower growth in 2008 than in previous years due to changing weather conditions, specifically rising temperatures, so the people are drinking less hot drinks. The real value growth is seen to be less dynamic compared to the reviewed period. Consumers are seen to trade down and remain more conservative in their purchasing decision which hampers real price growth. Tea as always enjoys the highest consumption level with teabags performing the best due to rising use of tea bags in offices. Coffee saw good growth in fresh coffee due to increasing coffee shops that use fresh coffee more now than any other type of coffee.

Even in the days of serious political crises nothing could hinder these companies from growing and yet they became successful. A major reason behind this is the nature of the product (coffee) that is affordable by anyone no matter what income group he or she belongs to. The Demographic changes as well didn't have any negative impact on this industry since coffee target all genders and age groups.

Market And Major Anticipated Trends

Coffee growth looks promising in light of increasing foodservice sales which is creating a coffee culture in Pakistan. This is coupled with the increasing number of instant coffee products available in the retail arena. Tea on the other hand will perform better as a refreshing drink to help consumers cope with their busy lifestyles and rising stress levels in the forecast period. While Lahore's coffee scene is growing, Karachi's, Pakistan's largest city, has exploded. In Karachi alone there are are currently 31 different coffee companies and CafÃƒÂ © Coffee Day, India's largest retail coffee shop chain, plans to open 19 more outlets across Pakistan in the next 12 months after the success of its first venture in Karachi. Moreover International Chains like Gloria Jeans has also opened 4 outlets in Pakistan due to the emerging coffee market in Pakistan.

The Indian-subcontinent, in particular Pakistan, has been a tea-drinking country since before the

British made tea popular in the West. Tea is consumed throughout the day and often served accompanied with "Samosas" and various sweets like "golabjamins" or cookies. Most offices have chai wallas or tea boys who serve workers multiple cups of tea during the course of the working day. On average, each Pakistani consumes about a kilo of tea a year, making approximately 140m kg of tea for a population of about 140m.

But all of that is changing. In the last few years Pakistan has seen an explosion in coffee lounges and cafes. Some are like your traditional Starbucks just serving coffee and snacks, while others are more all-inclusive cafes, serving coffee accompanied by proper meals. Pakistan is an emerging market for coffee. Coffee culture has been so fast in spreading its wings with new coffee outlets opening left right and centre in Pakistan. These coffee shops have played an important role in introducing coffee to the masses in Pakistan.

Now that coffee awareness has grown to such extent tea might finally have competition. Younger generation in Pakistan definitely prefers coffee over tea. This is not only because coffee is more hip than tea but also because coffee is more helpful in keeping energy levels going than tea ever has been. Professionals in Pakistan who need to be on the go for long hours are fast quitting the frequent tea breaks with fewer coffee breaks.

In the markets in Pakistan there are many varieties of instant coffee mixes available. Ironically now in Pakistan making tea is considered more difficult now that is how intensely coffee culture has taken over. In addition usage of coffee in everyday products especially bakery products has become very frequent.

In the more mature markets, the patterns of consumption have changed markedly over the last 10-12 years. The traditional, lower quality coffee products such as instants, are being replaced by roast and ground coffee (drips, plungers etc) and of course Espresso Based Drinks (cappuccino, latte, espresso etc). Fresh roasted coffee has many advantages over the instant coffee. It is more flavorsome and more importantly has a greater link back to where it originally came from. This means that customer awareness is also on the increase- bringing into the spotlight the actual paper trail of where the coffee comes from, who picked it, what price the grower get from it etc.

Coffee shops have become establishments where people are not only drinking coffee but also surfing the Internet, working from their laptops, or communicating with friends, family, and colleagues. Wireless technology is changing the way people live. Hotspots (Internet access areas that deploy wireless technology) can be found in airports, hotels, and coffee shops.

Some offer free access while others require paid subscriptions. Offering free wireless Internet in coffee shops is sure way to boost success. People are now given the option to make a connection over a cup of coffee and/or over the Internet.

21 DISTRIBUTION CHANNEL

Café Au liat has only one channel of distribution i.e. direct where the goods are transferred to the consumer directly. Café Au lait has no middlemen.

Distribution of consumer goods and services:

- Café Au liat would do distribution of consumer goods directly to the consumer.

- Café Au liat would also do distribution of services to the consumer like parking, sitting, home delivery, etc.

- CAFÉ au liat would get Wheels! Café Au liat would launch its first mobile unit, which took the streets of Islamabad by storm. The mobile unit has been designed to cater to the needs of those who are on the go, and have little time to stop by at cafe. It also provides a unique convenience of enjoying the delicious café Au liat offering anytime, anywhere, thus making fast food truly fast and convenient.

- Café Au liat intends to further develop its mobile network nationwide through more such units

Intensity of distribution

Café Au liat does intensive distribution on its outlets. (All and everything on the outlet)

22 THE CUSTOMER OR END USER

Café au liat strives to appeal to all ages. Young and Mature, all consumers are bound to be satisfied by their array of choices. The menu is designed specifically to cater to different preferences and the quality of their coffee satisfies the most discerning of tastes.

For the purpose of defining the target market, the following market segments were established after researching the restaurant and cafe-going consumers and the clientele of already established competitors.

Economic Profile:

   I.   *Middle Class*

   II.   *Upper Middle Class*

   III. *Privileged Class*

Age Groups:

   I.   *Teenagers*   *16 - 19 years*

   II.   *Young Adults*   *18 - 25 years*

   III. *Adults*   *25 – 50 years*

   IV. *Mature*   *50 and above*

Professional Classification:

   I.   *Students*

   II.   *Young Professionals*

   III. *Mature Professionals*

   IV. *Retired*

Marital and Familial Status:

   I.   *Single*

   II.   *Single with Dependants*

   III. *Married*

   IV. *Married with Children*

   V.   *Married with Dependant*

   VI. *Ethnic and/or Religious Classification: Christen, Muslim, Hindu Other*

   VII. *Asian, Caucasian, African American, Latin-American, European*

PRODUCTS

Café au lait will sell high quality specialty coffee beverages, tea, juice, water, soft drinks, pastries, chocolates and gift items. Despite being an upscale Cafe au liat, our prices are in line with the leading national chains.

The Café au lait Menu

The Café au lait menu sets us apart from other Cafe au liats, giving us a competitive edge.

- We offer six groups of drinks—coffee, tea, Italian sodas, smoothies, juice and cocoa—with several choices within each group. This enables us to provide more variety than our competitors while keeping the preparation of the drinks easy to execute.

- We are taking advantage of the immense popularity of flavored drinks and Chai tea by offering a product mix that includes items the other Cafe au liats don't carry as well as more familiar drinks.

- We are the only Cafe au liat to have a wide range of gourmet hot cocoa.

- Café au lait offers several smoothie drinks and Italian sodas.

- We carry the highest quality fresh juices.

Prices have been determined after a thorough analysis of all food costs for every item in each drink. In some cases, an average price has been calculated and applied to all similar drinks in order to keep the menu from confusing the customer.

23 IDENTIFY PROBLEMS AND OPPORTUNITIES

Problems:

- Presence of competitors in the market e.g. masooms, espresso lounge, hangout, and Yummy's.

- Imported raw material rise their prime cost

Opportunities:

- Cheap and easy availability of labor

- Increase consumption of fast food has increased the market size

- Consumer prefer "All under one roof" in order to increase their sales turnover they can increase or add the served items

Define Specific and Realistic Business Objectives

ASSUMPTIONS REGARDING FUTURE CONDITIONS:

Level of economic activity:

In markets in Pakistan there are many varieties of instant coffee mixes available. Ironically now in Pakistan making tea is considered more difficult then coffee, now that is how intensely coffee culture has taken over. In addition usage of coffee in everyday products especially bakery products has become very frequent.

In the more mature markets, the patterns of consumption have changed markedly over the last 10-12 years. The traditional, lower quality coffee products such as instants, are being replaced by roast and ground coffee (drips, plungers etc) and of course Espresso based drinks (cappuccino, latte, espresso etc). Fresh roasted coffee has many advantages over the instant coffee. It is more flavoursome and more importantly has a greater link back to where it originally came from. This means that customer awareness is also on the increase- bringing into the spotlight the actual paper trail of where the coffee comes from, who picked it and what price the grower gets from it, etc.

Level of industry activity:

Coffee growth looks promising in light of increasing food service sales which is creating a coffee culture in Pakistan. This is coupled with the increasing number of instant coffee products available in the retail arena. Tea on the other hand will perform better as a refreshing drink to help consumers cope with their busy lifestyles and rising stress levels in the forecast period. While Lahore's coffee scene is growing, Karachi's, Pakistan's largest city, has exploded. In Karachi alone there are are currently 31 different coffee companies and CafÃ ƒ Â © Coffee Day, India's largest retail coffee shop chain, plans to open 19 more outlets across Pakistan in the next 12 months after the success of its first venture in Karachi. Moreover International Chains like Gloria Jeans has also opened 4 outlets in Pakistan due to the emerging coffee market in Pakistan.

Changes in customer needs:

Pakistan had a tea culture even before British Empire colonized the subcontinent and with the advent of British rule it particularly became popular in Lahore. It is estimated that on average, each Pakistani consumes about a kilo of tea per annum, making approximately 140m kg of tea for a population of about 140 million. Tea is still largely consumed in Pakistan at breakfast, during lunch breaks at the work place and in the evenings. The tea culture is a century old tradition that has serpented its way in the hearts of many Pakistanis. But traditions are bound to change as time passes. With Pakistan having most of its population bracket comprising the youth, the tea culturally is gradually been replaced by the coffee culture influenced profoundly by the West. .In the last few years Pakistan has seen an explosion in coffee lounges and cafes. Some are like your traditional Starbucks just serving coffee and snacks, while others are more all-inclusive cafes, serving coffee accompanied by proper meals. Pakistan is an emerging market for coffee. Coffee culture has been so fast in spreading its wings with new coffee outlets opening left, right and centre in Pakistan. These coffee shops have played an important role in introducing coffee to the masses in Pakistan.

Now that coffee awareness has grown to such an extent, tea might finally have competition. Younger generation in Pakistan definitely prefers coffee over tea. This is not only because coffee is more hip than tea but also because coffee is more helpful in keeping energy levels going longer than tea ever has been. Professionals in Pakistan who need to be on the go for long hours are fast quitting the frequent tea breaks with fewer coffee breaks.

Changes in distribution channels:

Coffee cafes have become establishments where people are not only drinking coffee but also surfing the Internet, working at their laptops, or communicating with friends, family, and colleagues. Wireless technology is changing the way people live. Hotspots (Internet access areas that deploy wireless technology) can be found in airports, hotels, and coffee cafes. Some offer free access while others require paid subscriptions. Offering free wireless Internet in coffee shops is sure way to boost success. People are now given the option to make a connection over a cup of coffee and/or over the Internet.

Changes beyond our control:

Changes in marketing strategies are beyond control and one has to adopt them in order to compete in the market.

PRIMARY MARKETING OBJECTIVES

- Growing the profitability, scale and market share in the Pakistani market;

- Developing new products that have the potential to reach significant scale;

- Managing our business so that shareholder value is added by each of our activities;

- Ensuring that brand is a leader in its field for customer service;

- *"We will dominate every place in Pakistan where coffee is sold"*

- Working to meet our responsibilities to the wider stakeholders in our business, including commercial partners and the communities in which our brands operate.

OVERALL STRATEGY TO ACHIEVE PRIMARY OBJECTIVES

The overall strategies to achieve primary objectives will be:

- Superior-tasting products and a diverse menu.

- A relaxing, upscale Classic French interior design

- Prime site selection with an upscale affluent population, year-round tourist activity, heavy pedestrian traffic by the site, a dynamic student population and a concentration of local businesses

- A market that exposes Café au lait to high-profile "trend-setters" and "key influencers"

- Ongoing, aggressive marketing

- Highly trained and friendly staff

- Multiple revenue streams including gift items, gift baskets and coffee gift/frequency   cards in addition to coffee, pastry, chocolates, tea, juice, water and soft drinks

- A dynamic website with online sales capability

- To achieve the vision and primary objectives of **Café au lait** *"We will dominate every place in Pakistan where coffee is sold"* we shall continue using the same method of slow-roasting coffee beans that is unique to **Café au lait** to this day. The focus will be on quality control at every stage of the coffee making process from bean to cup. Unlike any other coffee company in the Pakistan, **Café au lait** has its own roastery to ensure their unique blend is perfect every time. The customer can order a cup of **Café au lait** today; it is made skillfully by hand rather than by the automated coffee machines used by major competitors.

FUNCTIONAL OBJECTIVES

Advertising Objectives:
With the expected growth of the billion dollar of our venture, Café Au lait is poised to capture a bigger share of the market with an aggressive marketing strategy.

Customer Service Objectives:
Short Term Goals: Improve market presence by 20% Short-Term Objectives Aggressive Marketing Strategy Café au lait can take advantage of the positive press on the health benefits of coffee to boost the sales of its coffee product line.

The company can use recent studies on the health benefits of coffee as the basis of its press releases and advertising campaigns.

Product Modifications Objectives:
Café Au liat has extensive research facilities on product improvement. The company can use its resources and professional expertise to come up with new flavors that will suit the continuous demand for healthy coffee for its customers.

New Product Objectives:
Our goal is to be the Cafe au liat of choice for people of Islamabad, downtown business workers, tourists who visit the city, and students, by providing a higher quality experience and exquisite Ambience than any other competitor. As a result, we intend to create Cafe au liats that quickly

achieve profitability and sustain an attractive rate of return (20% or more annually) for our investors. Furthermore, we would like to create a business and working environment where both the customer and employee are treated with dignity and respect.

Expense Control Objectives:

Profit - Personal income in excess of Rs.10, 50000 per year within three years

Clientele - create a base clientele of persons who live nearby and work in the area. These persons will like a relaxed atmosphere where they can "hang out"

Workforce Objectives:

Employees - Competent employees (at least 51% from low-income neighborhoods) who are committed and loyal

Personal Training Objectives:

Training to the labor that lacks skills required for operating the business.

Market Research Objectives:

Product Innovation café Au liat must continue its innovative research and development strategy to come up with new flavors and products.

24 Market Strategy

TARGET MARKET STRATEGY:

While evaluating their consumer market the conclusion was that the ideal consumer's economic profile will be

- **Upper Middle Class**
- **Privileged Class**

While the age demographics will comprise of :

- **Students and Youngsters**

- **Professionals**

- **Families**

- **Mature Consumers**

Gender and Ethnic/Religious Background was researched to have minimal or no effect on the choices concerning coffee made by consumers and their patronage of Cafe au liats.

25 MARKET SEGMENTATION STRATEGY:

- **Students and Youngsters** i.e. young men and women in the age bracket of 16-24 years are estimated to form 30% of the target market. This group will patronize **Café au lait** for the ambiance and the prestige as well as the delicious menu. Due to the burgeoning "Coffee Culture" in Pakistan, the youth is flocking towards Cafe au liats and cafes as their latest 'Watering Holes'. The luxurious environment and the image of class associated with **Café au lait** is bound to attract this group and make them a significant fraction of **Café au lait** potential clients.

- **Professionals** belonging to all careers and in the age bracket of 24 – 45 years are anticipated to form 45% of the future clientele. These will be up and coming, dynamic persons who will appreciate the mouth-watering menu, expeditious service and serious atmosphere. **Café au lait** is the ideal environment for efficient lunches and meetings from casual to semi formal to formal.

- **Families: Cafe au lait** 's menu caters to a variety of tastes and aims to satisfy all kinds of customers. Though a lesser percentage than Students and Professionals, we hope that consumers with families will make up 10% of the potential patrons. **Café au lait**'s wide array of scrumptious choices is designed to draw consumers of all ages: the melt-in-your-mouth, luscious desserts will without doubt make children love them while their parents can also enjoy the unique, delicious coffee; Making **Cafe au lait** a complete family experience.

- **Mature Consumer: Our mission is selling the best quality coffee with best services at every privileged place in Islamabad."** The trade mark is the exceptional quality and first class flavor. Who better than a matured, experienced veteran with discerning taste to appreciate the finer points of **Café au lait** The management hopes that Matured Consumers will comprise 15% of the potential clientele.

- **Market segmentation:**

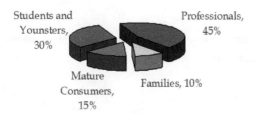

Students and Younsters, 30%

Professionals, 45%

Mature Consumers, 15%

Families, 10%

PLACE MARKETING STRATEGY:

Our first ventures in Islamabad are greatly anticipated and we intend to meet and go *beyond* these expectations.

Location:

After thorough research, and competitive analysis the perfect locations in terms of exposure, accessibility and competitive edge have been acquired.

Islamabad, due to its metropolitan way of life and culture and ideal market potential was chosen to be the launch pad for initiation into the market. A prime location in Jinnah super is to be renovated, designed and revamped according to the standard of **Cafe au liat.**

Other selected locations also include Jinnah Park (Rawalpindi) and Saidpur Village at (Islamabad). **Cafe au liat**plans to move to other cities of the country as well. All future locations of **Cafe au liat**outlets in Pakistan will be required to be the most conveniently located at the hub of cultural activity and possess the best competitive advantage.

The inventory and easy transport facilities have also been a part of the deciding factors while choosing the appropriate locale.

MARKET POSITIONING:

The quality of their coffee is better than the competitors- it tastes better; it is more hygienic and totally unique. The image of **Café au lait** is that it has the finest quality, unique coffee.

The position of **Café au lait**- for the upcoming market in Pakistan is the **Highest Standard of Luxury, the Best Service and a Reputation for Excellence**.

26 MARKETING MIX:

Brand Name:

Our brand name is our signature. The name of **Café au lait** signifies luxury, excellence and perfection. In today's market environment, along with quality, Image and Status are also all important. The quality and excellence that is **Cafe au liat** has made this brand name a trademark that is recognized and pursued.

Image/Theme:

Luxury and Comfort

The image of is **Café au lait** luxury. The theme has been designed specifically with the consumers in mind. The emphasis is on luxury and comfort- with style. The ambiance provided is trendy as well as soothing. The sobriety of **Café au lait** invites consumers to spend a pleasant time with their company without the tacky flash and glitter.

Color Scheme

The theme of, **Café au lait** from the brand logo, the color scheme of the premises, to the entire feel of our business is French tones & relaxing colors. The dominant color in the logo and the premises of **Café au lait** is green with touches of yellow and, brown. The color theme is chosen for relaxation & comfort as well as being upbeat & trendy and green shows that our organization is environmental friendly.

Service

Cafe au liats reputation for excellence applies not only for the exceptional coffee but also the insistence on perfect service. Recruiting and retaining highly motivated and talented people is essential and great emphasis is placed on improving the skills, expertise and performance of our people through award-winning, industry-leading training and developing programs.

PRICING STRATEGY:

Cafe au liat is to provide first-rate service, highest regard for quality and a determination to provide the best **handmade** *coffee* for the most discerning consumers in Islamabad.

The consumers appreciate these efforts and are loyal to. They will value **Cafe au liat's** commitment to their satisfaction and realize that luxury comes at a cost. A cost that will not deter them from pursuing the excellence of the coffee at **Cafe au liat**.

The prices of all the products are comparatively higher at **Cafe au liat**. But this is offset by the outstanding quality and discerning tastes at **Cafe au liat**. One of the reasons for choosing the privileged and higher middle classes in the target market is the prices.

PROMOTION:

Above and below the line Advertising strategies will be used to make **Cafe au lait** popular company. Due to limited financial resources, customers will be informed about this new venture through a TV ad which will run on Cable TV and not on big channels like Geo, ARY etc initially. At present Cable operators offer around about 7 movies on demand channels which are very popular amongst people in Islamabad. So the ad will run during the intervals and small trailers will also move on the downside of the screen to remind people about this venture. Huge emphasis would be given on making the advertisement i.e. "the message that it has to portray". Care would be taken of the fact that the ad is persuasive and attracts people towards consuming the products that are offered. Advertisement through Radio i.e. FM channels will also be done. Apart from this, fliers will be used to advertise the venture. Colorful attractive fliers containing persuasive information about the company and its products will be distributed in busy areas e.g. schools. These fliers will also be distributed in residential areas in almost all the sectors of Islamabad. Posters of our new venture will be pasted in all business areas especially outside bakery shops, utility stores etc. Small banners will be placed across Islamabad on all streets light towers especially on busy roads like 9th avenue, 7th avenue, Blue area etc.

Slogans and Punch line will be critically examined before their selection bearing in mind their importance in building customer retention of the advertisement. An emotional appeal will be made to the customer through slogans and other advertisement information.

Sponsorship and Prize schemes are the other ways through which promotion will be done. Focus would be given to sponsoring events organized by students in the universities and colleges e.g.

seminars, marketing events etc to catch the attention of general public and the higher officials from different professional fields who are invited as guests in those events. Prize schemes like Lucky Draws will also be held to popularize the venture and increase sales.

Hence gradually as the venture will become popular advertisement strategy will be upgraded. TV ad will be run on most popular channels like GEO and ARY. Print media like newspaper and magazines will be used to promote our products and in other words promotion will become more aggressive as time will pass.

27 MARKET DEMAND / OPPORTUNITY MEASUREMENT

Before expanding into any market, its opportunities and risks have to be analyzed. Smart Business is to venture into markets that have opportunity for profit maximization. The attractiveness of any market depends on the certain factors that have to be duly considered before launching any new project and even after launching it to continue a balanced growth of the market share.

28 PRODUCT FORECASTS

The Production department will be held responsible for Research and Development. They will be held responsible for bringing in new ideas from the international and local market. They would be allowed to do experiments. Failure will be allowed only if they come up with something really beneficial later on. In other words a huge responsibility will be laid on the shoulders of this department to introduce new product lines.. Customer surveys will also be used to make changes in the product line by including new products.

29 CONTROLS:

Performance of the venture and each of its products will be reviewed after every 3 months to apply product mix expansion or product mix contraction strategy.. New flavor would also be introduced based on the customer demand. Performance of the manufacturers will be reviewed e.g. how many hours they worked compared to how much they had to work, did they waste any raw material during production etc. Inspection will take place regularly to ensure that no one deviates from the quality standards. Decisions will be made regarding whether to continue with the existing suppliers or not. In simple words each possible step will be taken by the management of **Cafe au liat** to control the operations of the company.

In the first month of operation Management will over view that whether the Marketing goals and objectives are going in right direction or not if not than what went wrong and what are differences

between actual and expected performance. This may require changing the action programs or even changing the goals.

Operating control

It involves checking ongoing performance against the annual plan and taking corrective action when necessary. It will ensure us that the com-any achieves the sales, profits and other goals set out in annual plan. It also involves determining the profitability of product. • Strategic Control It involves looking at whether the company's basic strategies are well matched to its opportunities. Marketing strategies and programs can quickly become out-dated and there will be need of periodically reassess its over all approach to the market-place. A major tool is marketing audit.

Marketing Audit

There will be a need of monthly marketing audit regarding current activities and sales volume. It will cover all the marketing areas of business. It will include audit of: 1. Marketing Environment 2. Marketing Strategy 3. Marketing Organization 4. Marketing Systems 5. Marketing Mix 6. Marketing productivity 7. Profitability Measuring and Managing return on Marketing Investments

After six months of operation we have to measure that whether our investment is being spent well or not? Are we getting targeted Return on Investment or not? Return on Investment The net return from a marketing investment divided by the costs of the marketing investment. It measures the profits generated by investments in marketing activities. (Source principles of marketing) The consumer purchase decision process variables situation influences Psychological Purchase Social Need motivation solving problem solving Routine problem Extensive Economic Needs Search for information on solution Evaluate alternatives and decide decision Purchase product Postpone Post-purchase evaluation.

Printed in the USA
CPSIA information can be obtained
at www.ICGtesting.com
LVHW092145200824
788828LV00033B/317